MY BIGGEST QUESTIONS ABOUT GOD

Tony Evans

Illustrations by Jessica Blanchard

HARVEST HOUSE PUBLISHERS
EUGENE, OREGON

Published in association with the literary agency of Wolgemuth & Associates

Cover and interior design by Jessica Blanchard

For bulk, special sales, or ministry purchases, please call 1-800-547-8979.
Email: Customerservice@hhpbooks.com

This logo is a federally registered trademark of the Hawkins Children's LLC. Harvest House Publishers, Inc., is the exclusive licensee of this trademark.

My Biggest Questions About God
Text copyright © 2023 by Tony Evans
Artwork copyright © 2023 by Jessica Blanchard

Published by Harvest House Publishers
Eugene, Oregon 97408
www.harvesthousepublishers.com

ISBN 978-0-7369-8383-9 (hardcover)
Library of Congress Control Number: 2022944835

Printed in China

23 24 25 26 27 28 29 30 31 / LP / 10 9 8 7 6 5 4 3 2 1

Knowing God is the most
important thing you can do.

That's why it's such a great thing
to learn all you can about Him.

WHO IS GOD, AND WHAT IS HE LIKE?

The Bible tells us that God has always existed. It also tells us that God is a Spirit. This means we can't see Him, but God showed us what He is like by sending Jesus.

God is everywhere. Wherever you go—down in the deepest ocean, up to the highest mountain, or even out to the farthest stars—He is there.

WHO AM I,
AND WHY DO I EXIST?

God says, "I am with . . . everyone who is called by my name, whom I created for my glory, whom I formed and made" (Isaiah 43:5,7).

God made us to be like Him. Our purpose is to show and tell others about how great God is.

WHERE DID THE WORLD COME FROM?

"In the beginning God created the heavens and the earth" (Genesis 1:1). God created everything: the sun, the stars—all of it.

God created the world with His words. He said, "Let there be light." He spoke, and land and oceans appeared. Lions and tigers and giraffes and everything else showed up because God spoke them into being.

HOW CAN I FOLLOW GOD?

The Bible tells us that everything we do—like choosing good friends, listening to our parents, and showing kindness to others—can reflect God's glory.

God tells us how to follow Him: "Make every effort to live in peace with everyone and to be holy" (Hebrews 12:14). From when you get up in the morning to when you go to bed at night—and all the time in between—make sure you are obeying God's Word.

HOW CAN I KNOW THAT GOD EXISTS?

The greatest proof that God exists is the world itself. "Holy, holy, holy is the LORD Almighty; the whole earth is full of his glory" (Isaiah 6:3).

You see signs of God in the sun, moon, and stars and in the trees, plants, and animals. Wherever you go, you will find God's handiwork.

WHY DO BAD THINGS SOMETIMES HAPPEN?

Because God loves us, He gives us the freedom to make our own decisions. Sometimes we make good choices, and sometimes we make poor choices.

If we choose to go against God's Word, we open the door for sin. But when we ask God to help us, we open the door to His goodness.

WHAT DOES IT MEAN
TO GIVE GOD GLORY?

When we cheer and clap for someone, like an Olympic gold medalist, we give them glory for what they have done. The Bible encourages us again and again to glorify God for who He is and what He has done.

"LORD, our Lord, how majestic is your name in all the earth!" (Psalm 8:1). Every part of God is perfect; every part of Him is glorious.

WHAT IS THE TRINITY?

God the Father, God the Son, and God the Holy Spirit are called the Trinity. But all three of these persons make up just one God. It's like a pretzel with three holes. The first hole is not the second hole, and the second hole is not the third hole, but they're all part of the same dough.

HOW AM I A PART OF GOD'S PLAN?

God has a wonderful plan for all of creation. And because He is God, we can be sure that He will accomplish everything He wants to do. Nothing can stop Him!

God invites all of us to join Him in the great things He is doing. Imagine that—you get to be a part of His amazing plan!

IS GOD IN CONTROL OF EVERYTHING THAT HAPPENS?

God is in control of everything. Nothing surprises Him. He knows about everything and uses all things for our good. If something occurred, He either caused it or let it happen.

"The LORD does what pleases him, in the heavens and on the earth, in the seas and all their depths" (Psalm 135:6).

WHAT IS PRAYER?

The Bible tells us, "Pray without ceasing" (1 Thessalonians 5:17 ESV). Sometimes we talk to God at set times—like saying grace at the dinner table—and sometimes we pray throughout our day—like saying "Help, God!" when we're scared or worried. We can talk to God when we walk, think, or even ride in the car. We can talk to Him all day long! He loves to hear from us.

WHAT DOES IT MEAN FOR GOD TO BE HOLY?

Do you have a special room in your house? Maybe you don't eat ordinary meals in your dining room. You save that room for guests, birthdays, holidays, and important occasions. When we say God is holy, we mean that He is set apart and special.

Holy means perfect or pure. God's love is holy. His truth is holy. His Word is holy. His ways are holy. His name is holy. Everything about God is holy!

HOW IS GOD LOVE?

"God is love" (1 John 4:8). God has always been love! Everything He does flows out of His love. Through love, God created the world and gives us water, food, family, friends, shelter, and even the air we breathe. But most importantly, "God shows his love for us in that while we were still sinners, Christ died for us" (Romans 5:8 ESV).

HOW CAN I SHOW GOD'S LOVE TO OTHERS?

The Bible says, "Dear friends, since God so loved us, we also ought to love one another" (1 John 4:11). We can do that in lots of ways, like paying attention to people, smiling at them, and showing that we care about them.

God loves watching you share His love with others!

Made by God — with love.

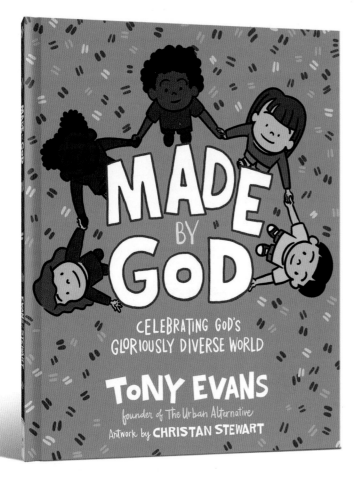

Equality. Diversity. Unity.

These are not just cultural buzzwords. They are all true reflections of what God's love looks like.

Dr. Tony Evans introduces children to these important values from a biblical perspective and equips you to have meaningful family discussions about race, reconciliation, and God's plan for all humankind.

TonyEvans.org